MW01228883

INTRODUCTION

Many people grew up thriving on the stories of the sweet and knowledgeable Mother Goose.

Her stories shaped thousands of minds, they helped to mold and build character in young children all over the world. She told wonderful childhood stories that told of the goodness in the world. This provided a manual on how to overcome childhood fears and how to show their strength in many ways. These are the stories that shaped a generation of minds.

The story's told by the Dark mother are the exact opposite of good. Where sweet Mother goose brought hope, the Dark mother will crush it. These stories are different; in these stories you will read of the darkness that creeps in the world. The darkness that lurks in the darkest parts of the human soul.

Follow the Dark mother on this adventure learn the truths that hide in the pretty lies we all know so well.

Acknowledgment

The Dark Mother is the first part of a three-book series, she is a branch of a very old tale, the tale of fate. Many people believe that, we are dealt a hand in life that we must play.

Whether that is a good one or not. What most people fail to realize is that life hands every one a crappy hand.

We are only granted the choice on how we will handle the

storms that come with the hand we are dealt.

The dark mother is the embodiment of what could become. A twisted soul that fed into the betrayals of life and accepted the darkness that so many see on a day to day basis.

She teaches us that feeding into anger and hate can change the course of our lives without necessarily changing how we got there.

But what she fails to see is how the untethered soul can never become unraveled, even in the darkness it is firmly tethered to its own fate.

Fate always comes balanced with all the bad there will be some good.

I wrote this book for that very reason, I wanted to shine a light on what could be. Give a voice to so many that have lived in their darkness, with the strength to never give life to it.

There is a strength to being resilient, a silent gift that we find a curse. I hope to inspire those with no voice to speak life into the dark.

Flick the switch and bring in the light that you so desperately need.

This series is for all the little girls stuck in a toxic cycle,

Just because life dealt you a crappy hand, that doesn't define who we are. How we deal with that hand is what transforms us into the goddess that is us.

*Unleash your pain and hurt
and step into your time of love
and light.*

WHEN MONSTERS MEET

(CONTAINS VIOLENCE AND SEXUAL ASSAULT CONTENT)

Her skin was that of caramel, her hair soft and free flowing. Her beauty was that of pure magic accompanied by grace and elegance. A flaw in the great design allows for men to take from the woman that gives him life, while also giving the opportunity to eradicate the beauty that she brings into the world. But like so many tales this one is balanced with darkness and hate. because what is humanity if it does not hold greed and desire at it's core?

In this story we are introduced to a beauty of the highest caliber, a young, widowed girl living in the 19th century. Left to struggle in life with less then a month to find balance for her unborn child.

Her beauty and kindness is matched by that of the opposite gene a male warlock with the taste for blood. For years he finds himself walking the earth fighting the inner demons that feed his thirst. While others bury their desires, he thrives off of his. Constantly giving in changing the lives of those around him.

It had been years since he felt the pull of the angry wolf that dwell hidden inside his dark soul.

Obliviously he surrounded himself with the humans, thinking he no longer was held captive by the beast that pledged his life for so long. But is that not how so many monsters think? For the darkness that brings them joy is what brings destruction to others.

Anger, fear and love resided in soul, it was on this day as he sat contently in an old restaurant he was presented with a beautiful young mother to be.

Some people believe that fate is just a fleeting feeling, one that can be pushed to the side and completely forgotten about. Others believe it to be an inevitable path, one that leads you to your own destruction.

Whatever you may think fate is, she is know in this story as Ebi a beautiful young mother bringing life into this world.

As he watched her serve the sailors, he could feel desire start to creep into his soul waking the beast he thought no longer resided within him.

He could feel the steady itch grow stronger and stronger, he tried to fight the idea from taking up space in his heart knowing that the only remedy was the smell of fresh blood filling the air, as he watched life escape the eyes of his beloved.

How could it be possible with all his years roaming this earth he has never had a pregnant woman. There it was the thought he tried so hard to fight, planting itself in his mind.

The excitement filled his belly with butterflies like that of a child on Christmas day. His saliva thickened as she got closer to his small round table. The tiniest glimpse from her forced him to quickly look away. He picked up his coffee cup in a lame attempt to look casual.

As she walked up to his table to get his order, his humanity showed itself. He could feel the smallest speck of guilt. How could he possibly kill a woman carrying a child? He thought to himself as he stumbled around her trying not to touch her baby belly.

As he ran down the broken boardwalk, he tried to focus on the pitter patter of his footsteps hitting the wooden beams that separated him from the ocean below. He struggled to drown out the voices in his head screaming for her death. He came to a sudden stop as he reached the edge of the dock. Bending over only to try and catch his breath.

His vision began to blur as the intensity of his urges began to consume him. He never felt the urge for death as strong as he did now. He sat his suitcase down and tried one more time to catch his breath. The sound of the waves crashing on the rocks began to settle him a bit. But the idea of blood would continue to resurface, taking over his mind.

He reached down at his suitcase and picked it up sitting it on the edge of the dock rail. He quickly opened it exposing the shavette within. He picked it up and placed the empty case back on the wooden dock floor. Taking one more deep breath he sliced his own palm; he closed his eyes as he felt his hand fill. The feeling of the soft velvet blood running down his fingers drew the voices to a standstill.

And then FATE! Almost as if all the forces of the universe knew something he did not. Ebi came wobbling over to him. Interrupting his tranquility. In a panic he quickly hid the razor under an old top hat he carried. He closed his eyes in disbelief how could this possibly be happening.

He thought to himself as he shoved his bloody hand in his pocket. Like a dam burst open the voices flooded his mind. They no longer were fooled by the dripping blood that was his own. They screamed for blood, and they would only settle for hers.

The wind softly blew carrying the smell of lavender as it met his face. He closed his eyes contently taking it all in. Making it the longest second in years, bringing it all to a calm.

Her soft voice sliced through the silence fast forwarding time, "Sir you forgot your rain jacket."

Her body filled with an uneasiness she knew something

was not right but she did not want to risk being rude and so she extended her arm, "Here take it."

A deep fog appeared out of nowhere moving in quickly as fear began to replace her feeling of unease, she dropped the jacket and turned to run. But he was much faster quickly overpowering her as he covered her mouth. Before she could fight, he already had the shavette in his bloody hand as he tore through her pharynx. Immediately he could feel her body tighten as she senselessly clawed at his hands exposing her abdomen.

Without a thought he reached down and carved away at her midriff. The sound of her blood hitting the old wooden beams echoed into his soul as she dropped into his arms. He watched as the life drained from her eyes. Soaking in every moment, at this moment there was no one else but him and her. As the fog he took one last look at the beauty laying in his arms and with a heavy heart he scooped her up and walked down to where the ocean kissed the sand. It was here that he released her body so that the ocean could carry her away.

It was not until he watched the last of her body sink that he realized he still had her child to dispose of. He quickly ran out of the water and back onto the dock unaware as to what condition he would find the tiny corpse.

Laying on the dock he found a small female child covered in her mother's blood. He picked up the tiny human and took a long deep breath; taking in all the smells that came with her fresh untouched skin.

He looked out over the ocean and whispered, " Thank you Ebi."

Suddenly a dark cloud covered the town, the streets empty with only the ghost to roam the streets. The winds slammed onto his body pushing and pulling him closer and closer to the water. It was very apparent the sea was angry, the waves crashed against the docks sending screams of rage through the air.

He could here the sound of female voices echo his name, " Sir Donnell" these voices where not that of the beauty that he fed to the sea. The figures of woman made of water started to fill the streets. It was as if Hades himself had taken over the town.

A giant wave swept over him knocking the child from his hands to the human eye it looked as if the child was lost to the sea. It was then that something else filled the air something monstrous. He moved defensively in a circle trying to get a clue as to what was coming.

This was something different, this monster brought him real fear. A fear he never experienced. He ran back to the dock in hopes to somehow get a glimpse as to what was coming.

Now you are probably thinking why not just leave? Why would

he want to see what is coming for him? Well because like all monsters Sir Donnell fancied himself invincible, there was no way he could not handle what was coming for him.

Standing on the dock he was greeted with waves shaped like giant hands flooding every street in sight. The storm howled like coyotes the water cut his skin like tiny knives leaving open wounds on his face and hands. Allowing the salt access to his sting his eyes and skin like a million wasps.

In the midst of the storm stood a woman full of fire and fury. Her hair no longer flowed with the wind but twisted and swirled in a whirlpool of hate and on her head she wore a crown of vengeance. Her cold, blue eyes pierced his evil soul as he finally realized who it was that stood before him.

Her anger filled the air with poison choking him from the inside out. When she lifted her hand a whirlpool surrounded him keeping him from running. " Tell me Sir Donnell, for how long will the men of this world walk among us thinking they are the Gods? Tell me when the world will see the worth of their women? I have watched you for many years take from this world beauty after beauty. The evil that resides in your soul takes the face of many, but I AM FATE! And you will not fool me!" Her mouth opened only to reveal a army of horses formed with water charging to consume the evil that faced the world.

As she turned to return to the sea the waters began to calm causing the storm to come to an end. The waters that filled the streets flowed back to where they came. As the town people came out their homes it did not take long for the first cry of horror to echo across the suddenly silent town.

In top of the small diner laid the body of Sir Donnell, his intestines wrapped around his neck. His arms and legs dismembered from his body and laying in his hands laid two eyes black as coal.

All eyes were focused on the display on the roof; all but one. A woman in the crowd slowly made her way to the edge of the water to lay a rose in revenant, "thank you sweet goddess of vengeance." Just

like a goddess a small child
washed up beside the woman.

The grateful woman reached
down and picked up the child,
"A curse I suppose so that his
spirit may wonder the earth
unable to ever find the way to
peace. Come little one so that
we may make your momma
proud."

The Beauty of Sin

(contains sexual assault and SI content)

Sin eaters have wondered the earth for centuries, risking their souls to soak up the sins of the dead. Town after town they roam looking to relieve sinners of their past transactions. What is not spoken of is the most powerful of all the sin eaters, an Irish settler that bore the name Celin.

She came to these lands as a powerful witch that carried the gifts of healing and empathy. Her beauty surpassed many, her head dressed with long red locks that twisted and curved as the roots of the trees.

Her eyes a blazing green that only can be compared to a fresh summers grass. Giving her the ability to cut right to your soul.

Her skin tightly pressed against her bones carried the color of a soft pink rose. Driving every man in the village to lust after her.

Celine unlike the other women in the village did not desire to be loved by a man. Her love lied in helping the sick. She passed her days bandaging the cuts of the children, her evenings reserved for the wounded soldiers that protected the village from unknown creatures in the night.

One night as she prepared for her bath she was struck from behind, knocking her unconscious. When she awoke her soft pale legs where bruised, the letters H A R LO T carved down each leg.

Both of her wrist bleeding from a slit running left to right. To cover up the atrocious crime committed. Her beautiful red locks drenched in her own blood, her pale skin now black and bruised. But the worst of all the crimes was the theft of her purity, the purity that sourced her healing magic. A condition given to her by the creator.

Across the room laid the lifeless bodies of three of the orphans that would often find comfort in her home. When she awoke to see all the pain that laid in her once loving home hatred filled her soul. Giving her the strength to pick up her naked, broken body off of the cold floor.

She took hold of her dark red robe and wrapped her body with it. She then proceeded to where the children laid picking each one up and carrying their tiny bodies to the middle of the floor.

Placing candles in a circle around the three children she recited this prayer, " I give easement and rest now to the dear children that lay before me. Come not down the lanes or in our meadows. And for thy peace I knock down my own soul."

Tears ran down her face as anger filled her heart, it was on this night she vowed to never let another one of these so called Christians die in peace. " with this fire I vow to always take the sins of the innocent but cast out the hate of the unworthy so that they may forever walk the earth in an endless daze never to know peace."

She made this vow as she set her home on fire watching as everything, she ever loved was consumed by dancing flames that warmed her face.

A figure dressed in a black cloak that reached the ground moved gracefully toward her; Behind every step he took a flower instantly bloomed. When he spoke his voice echoed through the forest causing the ground to shake. " My daughter it looks as if your vow to me was broken; for this reason I must take back the power that was granted to you."

Celin dropped face down at the feet of the creature in tears, " creator and great father please have mercy on me, do not take from me the gift you have bestowed on me for I did not break my vow willingly, instead transform my gift so that I may cast my revenge upon those who have stolen my virtue."

The creator stood in silence as he allowed for Celin to continue her plea, " great father allow for me to be able to take the sins from the innocent and reject the evil. Allow for me to become what keeps the evil from reaching your doors."

" My child, the gift you ask for comes with a great price, Negative energy has to be contained it must go somewhere. For every sin you consume you will be pledged with it. Forced to hold it within yourself for the rest of your days. Not only will it hunt you; it will corrupt your soul eating away all that is good within you. Are you so willing to pay that price?"

" I am willing to pay whatever price I must pay in order to clear the earth of the evil that calls itself Holy. Do you not wish justice for all the wrong that is caused in your name? Do you not wish for the men of this world to pay the ultimate price for the sins they have committed?"

" My daughter you have always been kind and fair, I see the brokenness the sins of these men have caused you; and it is for this reason I will grant to you, the wish you so vigorously ask for. But I must warn you once more, every sin you consume will stay with you causing you to become consumed by every evil you take on.

But, because of who you have been I will allow for you to pass this gift on to another. the next must also be born with the power of empathy, and of goodness. This sin eater will allow you the chance for redemption, they can take on all the sins that you have already consumed keeping those sins from walking the earth while also allowing your spirit peace. For every sin eaten there must be an offering this allows for there to be an open exchange of power. My child please take heed to my warnings, do not walk this earth for the rest of your days being the only sin eater. Seek out the next empath and set yourself free of the sins of the world."

Celine agreed to the terms of the creator opening the path of the sin eater's curse. Although she agree she never intended on passing on the gift with her dark magic she lived many years traveling from town to town looking for the ones that called themselves Holy.

After many years Celine found herself in the presence of a priest. Father Curtis was the man she searched so many years for. Only to find him living among the people he so hated. Like many animals he did not remember the pain he caused with his selfish desires. Nor did he wish to change his ways. Celine spent many years wondering how she would rip him apart but no death ever really seemed good enough.

No an animal of this caliber needed a truly awful punishment, " Father Curtis, I have looked for you near and far I pray that I am received with generosity and kindness as is your custom is it not?" she could see the lust in his eyes as he stood to his feet to examine the beauty before him.

" A woman as elegant and beautiful as you surely does not travel without a male companion to protect her."

"My Lord my companion is but two day behind, when I heard you where so close by I could no longer wait. I traveled ahead in hopes to get an audience before you return to the main lands."

The Father gave a small smirk and she knew that he was still the monster she knew so long ago.

"Come let us eat and conversate I am sure you are tired from you long journey." Just then a poor villager busted into the clergy house. "Father, please forgive me for the intrusion my boy is but eight years old he has fallen from a tall tree, the physician has only given him but a few minuets of life. Please Father come and give the Sacrament of the

Anointing of the sick; so that my boy may pass in peace."

This was it, almost as if the creator was opening doors so that she could hurry and finish the job. "I can not give the Anointing, he is not sick but he has injured himself this is between him and God now." Celin smiled with satisfaction, " You Holy men never change, you are so worried about getting me alone to try and violate me that you would allow for a small innocent child to die tortured by his sins. Come sweet mother I am the Sin eater known as Celin I can rid your child of his sins so that he may meet our creator in peace. There is a small payment of a piece of bread shared with the dead will that be available?"

"ARE YOU INSANE!!!!! SIN EATING IS DARK MAGIC AND WITCHCRAFT!!!! YOU WILL BE PUT TO DEATH FOR SUCH TREASON!"

Celin stood up straight with pride, " I would rather meet my creator with a clear conscious then live a life covered in the filthiest of all sins. Tell me Father which is the purest of souls, is it the one who gives an innocent child rest or is it the evil that tortures and rapes the weak in the name of his faith?"

She quickly turned and ran with the mother to see the small boy. She quickly dropped to her knees as she broke bread upon the child, "I give easement and rest now to this dear child that lay before me. Come not down the lanes or in our meadows. And for thy peace I knock down my own soul."

Celine has been doing this long enough now that she could identify each sin for what it was she looked over at his mother and smiled, " I hope it brings your heart piece to know that the sin your son carried was stealing apples from the tree you fell from."

The mother cried, " we have very little to eat here and his little brother's birthday is only two days away. He wanted only to make him an apple Danish."

Celine's heart was full something that does not always happen when she gets to use her power, " your sweet boy is with the creator now in the land of peace."

As she left the small cottage she was greeted by a group of "Holy" shoulders, " In the name of the Almighty you are under arrest for practicing Witchcraft."

They quickly chained her bringing her in front of the church council Father Curtis stood to his feet, "you are accused of practicing the dark magic of sin eating what do you plea?"

Celine opened her big green eyes and gave an evil smile, "I am a Sin Eater much like your Jesus once unlike him I also posses other forms of magic. So, I say to your Father Curtis you are accused of Rape, torture and brutally killing hundreds of innocents in the name of your Religion how do you plea?"

"TAKE THIS BLASPHMAIS
SHE DEVIL TO BE BURNED
AT THE STAKE AT
ONCE!!!!!"

Celin gave a hard laugh, "so
nice of you to make my job
easier before I go, I have but
one thing to say to the council,
On this full moon as the fires of
the earth consume me I cursed
all those that call themselves
Holy, for your cause you will
travel this world an outsider.
Filled with hate and emptiness.
Forever wondering the world
looking for your true purpose
never finding what your heart
longs for. With my last breath
Great creator, I release the sins
of all the great evils I have
collected. Scorching their
grounds and poisoning their
cattle all the sun to never
nourish their skin or give
strength to their children.

With their hands no life will come to full term, no water will quench their thirst, and no food shall fill their bellies. While you believe you have won, know this oh Holy Father I am cursed to walk this earth until the next sin eater comes of age!"

In a cloud of smoke, she disappeared as quickly as she came.

Tell me friend, are you Holy or are you human? What makes one more so then the other? Who in all this madness was the teacher and who was the student?

We tend to forget the lure of the past for the tales of the present but there is wisdom in our history waiting to be unlocked. Do not be blinded by

the colors of the light for even
the light covers the sins made
in the dark.

To the Depths of Despair

(warning contains mental health, physical violence content)

People say they are making the world better by building computers and fancy new cars. But what they do not seem to understand is that with every new idea comes about an even uglier outcome. I remember a time when ji could step outside and the green leaves that hung on to the branches where a breath taking site.

A time when the sound of music inspired joy, happiness and even love. The smallest of pleasures had such a huge impact on ones life. I remember doing two weeks chores just to be able to buy a small piece of chocolate. Now it seems as though you could pick it off the polluted streets over used and under rated.

I grew up in a small town just outside of Lancaster Pennsylvania. My papi owned a little meat store on the corner while Mami took care of the small farm house I grew up on. When I was nineteen Papi shipped me away to New York to marry some puto from the military.

Every time of think about it I get filled with rage, but then I remember it wasn't papi's fault

I was fourteen when I fell in love with that gringo sucio. The gringo was almost nineteen when he came to work for papi and to be honest I liked the way he made me feel like a woman.

After a couple months of sneaking ice cream dates and rolling in the fields I started to sneak off to lay with him. I wanted so badly for him to marry me and make me his wife. A stupid idea for a stupid little girl. I ended up getting myself pregnant, the worst part is I never even knew I was pregnant not until Mami told me I was. For a while she kept it our little secret as she tried to figure out a way to explain it to Papi.

Finally one day Mami pulled me to the side to tell me she

found a way to take care of my baby problem without Papi ever knowing about it. She found her a bruja that supplied her with a potion made to help me extract the baby, whatever that meant.

The day came and as usual Papi had to run to town to tend to the meat store. The difference with this run was that he would be staying for a couple days at the store doing inventory to get things settled for our biggest season of the year.

Mami waited a hour after Papi left to make sure he did not forget anything once she was sure he was gone she pulled out the potion and made me drink it. Just like the bruja said the baby came right out, the problem with the potion was that it didn't take the life of the baby. He was alive, " Santa maria eperamo muy tarde" (Holy maria we waited to late to do this) Mami cried.

She stayed up all night trying to figure out a good way to break this to Papi when he comes back. when the day came Mami made me swear never to tell Papi that the baby was mine. She named him Jose and when Papi showed up at the house she lied and told him that we found the boy abandoned by an old well behind our house. Papi immediately loved baby Jose he always wanted a boy and he would always say how he was God's miracle to our family. I continued to sneak around with the gringo and when baby jose was about two years old I got the sickness again. This time

Mami was not happy to help
she kept telling me to leave that
gringo alone. Their kind
doesn't mix well with ours. But
I could not help myself I loved
him.

When I told him about this
baby, he decided that he could
not have a baby with me. "we
don't mix margarita" he would
say. You are a Spanish girl
from the working streets. My
father would disown me if he
ever found out we were
together I am to be married to a
woman of my own kind. I can
not be tied to a halfblooded
baby."

The hurt in my heart must of
traveled down to my belly
because it was on this day that
my little stella was born. She
came out different then Jose
she did not cry when she was

born, Mami said she was not breathing the cord that was meant to give her life was wrapped around her little neck choking her to death.

The look on Papi's face when he walked into the barn and saw my stella laying in the hay, was something I will never forget , " yo lo mato el gringo sucio ese. Ella es una nina!" (I will kill him that dirty outsider, she was just a child.) He took his riffle and started making his way to the store. Mami quickly running behind him begging him to stop and think, " we are not of this world you kill that white boy they will kill you and all of us along with you."

Her words stopped Papi in his tracks, she always knew how to handle Papi when he was on a rampage. But she wasn't ready for how he was going to respond to me. " You better find a way to make this wrong right or don't even think of stepping foot back into my house."

The shocked look on my face was very apparent when I look at Mami to help me. As expected to jumped at the chance to defend me, " No not my baby she is only a child you cant just put her out. It is just as much our fault as it is hers."

"Mujer!" He yelled as he lifted his fist to hit Mami. "NO PAPI NO!" I yelled " your right I will stay out in the barn until I can make this right." Mami ran over to hold me and I cried with despair. " how am I going to fix this Mami?" I asked she just shook her head, " I will figure it out just give me some time Mija."

I ended up staying two weeks in that dusty barn, just me and my baby stella. I would tell stella stories of the warriors from our island. Telling these stories over and over made it very clear as to what I had to do. I did not have a choice I had to make things right with Papi.

What kind of mother would I be if I let my baby live out her life in a freezing old barn?

The smell of the cows was unbearable, and it was starting to stick to stella's beautiful brown skin. She was always so cold, and it seemed her body only got colder and colder as the nights passed by. The dust and dirt were starting to turn her skin black, and she desperately needed a bath. Baby's are not meant to be in the cold you know they could get really sick.

I was a good Mama to stella I made sure she had enough love, support and kisses that any little girl could ask for. The best part of having a baby was that she looked exactly like me! She had the sweetest little cry; it was so low that only I could hear it. I think thought meant we were meant to be mother and daughter because with baby Jose, everyone could hear him crying.

Being the good mother that I was I knew I had to get stella into the house. I heard a couple weeks back that the gringo started working at the tanner's pig farm, feeding the hogs before the sun came up. One night I waited until stella fell asleep and I marched right up to the tanner's farm.

Once I reached the tanner's farm I waited until I saw the gringo start filling the buckets. It was now or never. I slipped off my sundress, washed my face with the horses drinking water and walked right up to him. When he saw me standing in the moonlight he started to assure me that we could not be together, but he would still be open to having some fun tonight.

I told him I always wanted to be taken in a slaughter den. I guess he thought since my father ran a meat market that it was not strange to say because like a stupido pendejo he took me right to the slaughter den. I laid with him right there and right before he was going to fill my belly with his offspring I grabbed the closest meat hook and gammed it right into the side of his neck.

I wanted to make sure he could not scream, having it already hooked it allowed for me to hang him. I grabbed a skinning knife and started with his arms and upper torso. The blood was everywhere, I could feel the blood cover my naked body like a red velvet jacket. I wont lie I liked the feeling so I gutted him, putting his skin on mine and wearing it until it turned cold.

The sun started to come up and the pigs started screeching,

asking for food so I did what any good person would do I fed the pigs and walked home.

When I got to papi's house I knocked on the back door but when he opened the door he looked frightened to see me. " Papi I did it, I took care of the gringo. Can I come home now?"

I never really could wrap my head around why he seemed so scared. Looking back at it now I don't think I could fully understand the extent of what it was I just did. I did not look at it as if I was wrong. Mami on the other hand was not ok with what I did, she seemed very upset as she turned to Papi and smacked his head, " Look what you did! Fix it!" she yelled as she turned and went inside to get me a towel.

Papi was in shock, " Come hija take a bath and get cleaned up before jose wakes up and sees you like this."

Mami was always a good mom, she supported me in ways that no one ever could. I was finally allowed to stay in the house but I would have to sneak into the barn to see stella. Mami said that Papi just would not understand why I still kept her and I did not want him to kill her. Stella understood I slept with her every night and during the days I was able to bring her food and fresh clothes. I was even able to sneak a water basin out a couple times to give her a bath.

During the warm days we would go on long walks together and have little picnics by the well.

By the time summer came around stella started to look kind of sick. So I did what any good mother would do, I found a way to make her better.

I started baby sitting for a couple that lived a few towns over. I had decided for stella's new look she would not be a brown girl anymore. This way I could bring her into the house with me. So on their fifth date when this lovely couple went out, I got to working on deskining the baby; I was hoping I would be done and out of the house by midnight before they got home.

But I did an even better job and was out by eleven, leaving me plenty of time to make it home. I worked all night in the barn laying out the skin; and getting it ready to be sown on to my stella. It took me one week to stuff and sow my baby together again. And on the last day Mami came to the barn to bring me dinner.

She was so curious to know what I had been doing up here for a whole week. As I sowed a small piece of my stella's hair into her new chest mami started with her questions. I never lie to my mami that is part of having a good relationship you know. Bu when I told her everything her face turned green. She started to cry as she held me close to her body.

By the end of that night Mami helped me with the missing stitching's and we took stella back to papi's house. Stella got a new body every year until she was five years old. But like all good things nothing last forever and when she turned five the police finally caught on to me.

I never thought I did anything wrong and to be honest I still don't understand why they wouldn't just let me take care of my baby like any mother would. It is because of this reason that they stuck me in this god forsaken place. Telling me that I am insane.

But the only thing that makes me feel crazy is not having my daughter with me. not knowing what happened to her, or who is taking care of her. I missed her every day terribly that is until a few years ago when I got a package from my Mami. Her card read " mi hija I have become very ill, los doctores have given me only one month to live. By the time you receive this letter I will already be dead, but even on my death bed I think of you and your sweet stella. In this box I send to you a piece of my love. I should of helped you more when I had he chance.

I feel as if I did not do enough for you in your younger years so enclosed is your sweet stella wrapped in me so that you may keep us both in your arms until your last days. I love you mi corazon."

Stella and I are inseparable now, with the perfect mother, daughter relationship thanks to her beautiful grandmother.

The Rambling's of a loved wife

(contains sexual violence and SI content)

If there is one thing in this world that does not lie, it is the soul. No matter who you are your soul will always be what it always was. Some people believe that inside of every person one can find a little bit of themselves. Human's are these weird creatures that are always fighting an endless battle between good and evil constantly trying to change their destiny. But if one really, truly and honestly looks within them are we not destined to be who we already are?

My soul is broken, it has always been broken I have always known since the beginning of my time that I was not whole. What I was created for is a question I was not always sure about. What I do know is that I have no moral compass my internal arrow does not always point North.

And on this night this fact is made very clear.

As I sit here waiting for my cheating husband to make his way home, I cant help but picture his hands running up and down her thighs like they once did mine. I can feel the tears start to run down my cheeks but not the sad or confused kind of tears. No these were born from anger and rage. I could feel as the rage started to take over and blind me. This man broke me he broke my soul; he did not break my heart or my spirit but my very soul. To make things worse he has the audacity to ask me to forgive him as if he just stole my last yogurt.

The anger that slept in my broken souls started to seep in through the rifts, controlling my hands and poisoning my heart; it forced my mind into complete and utter madness.

I heard as he walked into my room, I watched as he took his shirt off and sat down next to me on the bed. I could see his flapping gums but I could not hear any words fill my ears. I just stared at his handsome face trying to find my way out of the darkness that was taking control of my life. As I searched my mind trying to find the right words, " you should go" was would I look for but they were quickly replaced with, "drop your pants" like word vomit they just shot out.

It was so crazy, I felt as if my body was hijacked. I went from being the captain of my ship to a mere passenger unable to take the wheel. I watched as he stood up with this stupid look on his face. He look as if he just won some great victory, and this just fueled my madness some more.

I numbly walked over to his half naked body and dropped to my knees. He stood tall towering over my submission.

I'm sure he thought " this is how it was supposed to be." As I stick him inside of my mouth I hear as he whispers a silent and degrading, "yessss." Suddenly I watch myself bite down as hard as I can. His screams bring me back, giving me complete control of my actions. Except it is to late by this point in time I have gone to far I have to finish it.

So I bite down a little harder, I keep biting harder and harder until I feel my mouth fill up, like when you bite into a fruit gusher. Except this was not fruit and my mouth was filled with warm gush of copper and flesh.

By now he has switched from victor to victim mentality and has started to punch me in the head. With every punch I can feel the skin tear a little more, over and over until finally there is a snap. I look up and stand to my feet, he drops like a sack of potatoes his whole body is shaking in pain. I am sure he probably would be yelling but his jaw is clenched shut as he holds himself where his membrane was once attached.

I spit his membrane at him as I walked to the kitchen to grab the knife from the counter. After all I could see how much pain he was in and he was my husband it was my job to try and help get him out of pain right? As I got back into our room I turned him over so that he was laying on his stomach and not his back.

I know it sounds crazy but I still love him, he is going to die and I can not live without him.

I knew he just did not understand what was happening, but if he is dead and I am dead then he can not leave me. then our spirits could wonder the earth as gilded lovers together forever. Plus ghost don't cheat so we will finally be happy.

As he lays on his back so perfect, so handsome, and so wonderful I cant help but think how lucky I am to have him. Holding the knife in my hand I whisper, " do you still love me?" his bloody coughs give me a little cause for concern but finally he can speak, " you will always have my heart; now please call for help."

I joyfully smile as I plunge my knife deep into his chest cutting out his beating heart, " yes I will my love." I whisper as I

pull his still heart up to my lips
and kiss it softly. Now the time
has come my dear sister, you
will find me with two cut wrist,
on one hand I will be holding
my love and on the other his
heart. Know that as you read
this letter I leave this world
happy and loved.

The Safe Space

(mental health and violent content)

" In life we will die over and over again, until the day that we can walk the earth with only our immortality left." Teal Swan

As I sat in that cold room, on a hard wobbling chair I could not help but be stuck in my own head replaying that quote repeatedly. My whole life I was a no body, whether it was to my mother, father, sisters or brother no one ever remembered what it was that gem wanted. I was always put on the back burner, so much so that I actually started to like being forgotten about.

That is until I met him. He made life so much better so much easier, he stood up for me and made me feel like I had a voice. Flashes of his bloody corps lying on my kitchen floor continue to flash through my mind.

The job was so sloppy, sloppy enough to make me think it may have been an amateur kill. But I know better I play those tricks on cops all the time.

The wobbling of the squeaking chair snapped me back into reality as I looked up at the cop that was walking towards the empty table I was sitting at. I wiped the tears from my face and with a cracking voice dared to ask the stupidest question I knew, " did you find anything?" The officer lowered his head and softly responded exactly as I expected him to, " No ma'am, I'm so sorry. Can I ask if you know of anyone who may have been an enemy to your husband?"

I wanted so badly to start crying again, this must have been what people feel like when they are weak. My sister always told me not to get married, she always believed that loving Caleb would make me weak. She was right, all I wanted for so long was to live a happy life, to love and to be loved. She knew life was not made for people like us. We were meant to do things that others could not even fathom. With such a great responsibility the simple life just wasn't in the cards for me.

Ma'am the officer said as he broke my train of thought, " is there anything at all you may want to tell us to help in the investigation?" Still staring at the broken clock on the wall I answered, " yes, he just wanted a pie, I gotta get home and bake his pie; he loves my pies you know. Yea that's what im going to do make a pie." I said as I stood to my feet. The cop stood up with me taking a look into my cold dead eyes. I could see the concern on his face as he quickly looked away, " Ok ma'am we will contact you as soon as we find anything."

I nodded my head yes but deep down I knew they wouldn't find anything. I knew this because I was going to make sure they didn't. Whoever was responsible for this was not going to have the luxury of having a comtorble bed and three square meals a day. It did not matter who they are they will never be safe from my wrath.

Driving home was not an option for me, so I walked. I could not get the image of him out of my mind. I prayed that this was just a dream as I walked my little legs down the quiet streets of Minersville Pennsylvania. I was numb to the pain by now. I knew that the only way to get to the bottom of this was to figure it out myself. These cops didn't know what they were doing. Shit I should know I moved town to town murdering and killing the scum that walked this earth never once had they come close to finding me. I have never worried about what the police may or may not have known and I was not about to start today.

I quickly reached the long driveway that led to my little brick house, I will admit I had to take a pause for a second. Staring at the beautiful little house with all the lights on, gave me a small sense of comfort, almost as if I was expecting him to be sitting at the table ready to tell me about his day. For that split second I forgot I was living in my literal nightmare, and I allowed myself to remember the joy that once came whenever I pulled up to this driveway.

I closed my eyes and could feel his warm touch, I could feel the love that radiated from his fingers as he wrapped his hands around mine. I made the mistake of letting my mind run with the memory of love and I forgot just what was waiting for me inside that empty house. I joyfully ran to the door yelling, " Babe!"

Suddenly the blood splatters and pools interrupted my bliss shooting me back into a memory I don't ever recall having. I hated this memory, it made me feel sick to my bones, I really could not handle it so I did what any good wife would do I made up a new one.

I picked up the phone and I called the only number that my delusional mind could remember, my older sister. "Hello is that you gem, gem can you hear me?" she sounded frantic. I had no control of my mouth as I yelled out her name, " MEG, meg someone kidnapped Caleb we have to find him. Will you help me?" I begged but she knew what was about to happen so she cleared her throat and proceeded to speak, " Gem, Caleb is dead. They found his body in your kitchen, don't you remember? You just left the police station. You should not be in the house alone let me come pick you up."

"No I cant leave, I can't just leave him I have to find him Meg just help me." I could hear the anger in the base of her

voice as she snapped at me,
"Gem you are delusional!
Bring your crazy ass over here
or I will hunt you down and
drag you here. I am not afraid
to lock you up in the celler I
did it before. You don't even
know what happened what if
you are the one who killed
caleb? After all you guys where
fighting., didn't you say you
were thinking of getting a
divorce because he was closing
in on your secret?

Come home so I can help you,
I am your sister I wam the only
one who will understand you."

Before she could finish I hung
up the phone how dare she
insinuate that I was the one
who killed caleb. She was
always such a Bitch but there
was one thing she was right
about we where fighting and I

was going to file for a divorce. Could I have been who killed him? There isn't any evidence pointing to anyone. Could that be proof that I was the one who killed him and then covered it up? I violently shook my head, No way, I could but if I did Miranda would know she knows me better then anyone.

I picked up the phone and dialed Miranda's phone number, " Miranda, I think someone kidnapped caleb will you help me find him?" *My sweet little sister sounded so hurt and broken, sometimes she doesn't realize when her two worlds blur together. She has border line personality disorder and at times it is extremely hard to manage her.* "Yes Gem I will help you where do you think we should start?" she asked. I was all over the place to be honest. I didn't know where the first place would be to start, my thoughts where torn between hiding in this delusion that the love of my life could still be alive and the very real possibility that one of the two people that mean the world to me could be the killer.

I took a deep breath and swolled my pride, " Miranda I don't know what to think anymore, do you think I killed Caleb?" The very sentence nearly killed me I broke down in tears and dropped to the blood stained floor. I could hear Miranda on the phone calling my name, " Gem, gem, I'm coming Gem hold on don't lose control Gem."

By the time Miranda got to my house she found me covered in

Caleb's blood, I was still curled up in the fetal position crying like a newborn baby. " Oh Gem!" she cried as she ran over to pick me up. She grabbed my shoulders and pulled me closes wrapping me in her arms. " You are a complete mess, I promise you were not the one who killed Caleb, I promise you didn't. You Gem are to good heart and kind to ever hurt someone you cared about."

I held my hand out in front of my face, his blood was on my hands now and still nothing was adding up. The only thing I could do was bake a pie so I got up and baked a pie. As I stood there rolling out dough I could see myself out of my physical body. It was so strange, I literally could see a form of myself that I hadn't seen since high school. She looked right through me and said, " Look at you in shambles, you have covered yourself in this mans blood in a desperate attempt to convince yourself that you killed him and for what? So that you can take your own life? you stupid pitiful girl get your ass up. You already know who killed him don't keep allowing for love to weaken you. Be strong, get up go find her and make her pay!"

The flashes of that day flew through my head, the door was not broken into. That means it was unlocked or the killer had a key, or at the very least caleb knew the killer. They found his body laying face down meaning that caleb trusted the killer enough to turn his back to them. The killer is no amature, the killer knew

enough to cover up the scene
by making look like a amature
did it.

" She's the killer" I whispered.

.

.   .

" Death is not the greatest loss
in life. the greatest loss is what
dies within while we live."
Norman Cousins.

It has been a few days since I
realized who killed the love of
my life. I am moving past that
now I do not want to make my
story about some moronic love
story revenge plot. I got things
to do and places to be with no
time to mourn over a lost soul
that was never meant to be with
me.

People die everyday, I should know I kill them. One thing I have learned is that you can only kill something or someone that is weak and vulnerable, and I my friend an neither. I am now in my safe place. ......

Made in the USA
Columbia, SC
20 August 2024

c33cebe4-45ff-4810-9932-16951868b83bR02